Respect.

Book Of Dhi Love By Abhi DhiYogi

Copyright © 2024 NABROS & Partners LLC | DhiYogi Family + Foundation

NABROS & Partners LLC First Edition February 2025.

Special discounts are available for education and in need institutes plus bulk orders. An author event/concert may be requested. For permission and all other requests please contact:

Publications @ NABROS & PARTNERS LLC. , 4320 Winfield Rd: Suite 200, Warrenville, IL-60555, USA | iINVENTme.org | Email: hello@nabros.com | Phone: +1 630 796 7676

Printed and created in the United States of America. Library of Congress Cataloging-in-Publication Data is available.

PRINT ISBN: 978-1-963651-00-3

EBOOK ISBN: 978-1-963651-01-0

PREQUELS

---

iINVENT Manuscript:
To wake up your ideas

Book Of Dhi Yoga:
Ideas 1 to 108

Book Of Dhi Truth:
Ideas 109 to 216

CONTENT

THANK YOU

To the family I have
and the strangers I met along the way.
To each good experience
and the bad ones that led me a stray.
To my friends who were there when in
need and to those who showed me my
weak knees.
To the happy memories
and to the sad ones that made sure I don't
forget.
To the mother of all
and to the father I will meet one day.
I thank all of you for
the adventure of circles and the infinite
moments
in which we finally intersect.

Dec 7 2014 1 pm @1816zenden

ABOUT

Dhi is the essence within one which resonates with…

This resonance of ideas is an effort to compliment one's unique pursuit at work, school and home with Dhi Yoga to:
Balance in everything to catch ideas. Open up to all to plant the ideas. Learn the lesson in each experience, be it good or bad, to grow the ideas.

A good idea is one that helps us, others and the environment.

If fish are special because they have fins and birds are special because they have wings, us humans, we have the intellect to manifest ideas as our core strength.

Oct 16 2016 6 pm @1816zenden

A LETTER TO DHI

"As you embark on this journey called life,
remember, you do not have to
become anyone,
you were born a masterpiece,
you are the best and there is no one
else like you.
Taking one opportunity at a time
along the way,
whenever you give your best,
that best in you will be realized,
little by little.
And with each choice made,
you may face a resulting win or
loss, good or bad, yes or a no...

But, learning to share the lesson in
each experience
irrespective of the result,
will lead you to the best this life has to
offer.
Wishing you give the best and learn from
the rest
as you embark on this journey called life."

May 22 2018 2 pm @1816zenden

IDEA:

Are all ideas born out of Love?

For a lotus to bloom, it needs dirty
muddy waters.

DHI-217
Jul 1 2017 6 pm @1816zenden

One is at the depth one's awareness is.

DHI-218
Aug 4 2017 5 pm @1816zenden

When there is gold strewn everywhere,
one may start to think the few rocks and
pebbles one has accrued are the worthy
treasures.

DHI-219
Aug 9 2017 11 pm @1816zenden

Our mind is driven by desires.
Our heart is driven with Love.
And our breath is driven by Truth.

DHI-220
Sep 4 2017 9 pm @1816zenden

Did the chicken come first or the egg?

Everything is a circle.
If the starting point is considered as the
chicken,
then the ending point right next to it is
the egg.
If the starting point is considered as the
egg,
then the ending point is the chicken.

So what came first?
Dhi Love at the center of the circle came
first from which the circle of the egg
and the chicken originated with each
breath.

DHI-221
Sep 11 1 2017 1 pm @1816zenden

One's pursuit or the purpose or the "why" may change with time: from desire to Love to Truth.

Dhi is driven by desires from birth to adulthood.

Then Dhi is driven by Love up to mid life.

After which Dhi is driven by the Truth.

DHI-222
Sep 18 2017 11 pm @1816zenden

When the lotus grew from the mud, slush and murky waters to bloom and touch the sun,

It became aware of the truth within and everything around.

So, when the sun set,

It started the journey to it's root,

Because it realized,

The Truth within it is in the sun, sky, air, dirty waters and the mud.

It was just here to reflect

"The Truth" to all of those around it.

DHI-223
Oct 1 2017 9 am @1816zenden

The truth in the matter is hidden in
the mind.

The truth in the mind is hidden in
the heart.

The truth in the heart is hidden in
the breath.

The truth in the breath is hidden in
the moment.

When One becomes anchored in
the moment,

The truth in all: breath, heart,
mind and matter comes forth to life
with Love.

DHI-224
Oct 16 2017 11 am @1816zenden

When the mind anchors to the breath,

It becomes aware,

It responds vs react,

so as to do, speak and think the best ideas.

When the heart anchors to the breath,

It becomes aware,

To accept and open up to all

so Love may manifest.

When the awareness anchors into breath,

It becomes one with the One:

who witnesses the Truth manifesting into Love in the heart, and this Love manifesting into the best ideas in the mind.

DHI-225
Nov 4 2017 1 pm @1816zenden

The sky around reflects the sky in my Dhi.

The sun reflects the sun shining in my Dhi.

The air reflects the air I have in my Dhi.

The water reflects the water flowing in my Dhi.

The earth reflects the earth in my Dhi.

Or, vice versa may also be true.

DHI-226
Dec 1 2017 11 pm @1816zenden

Space is all prevailing and pervading:

It allows all manifestations: planets,
moon, sun and more,

And it carries the whole universe that it
manifested on its shoulders.

Looking at the sky when the space within
One is reflected,

One becomes aware of the
manifestations within.

DHI-227
Dec 12 2017 1 pm @1816zenden

With balance, mind hooks onto peace.

With openness, heart hooks onto Love.

With learning, the breath hooks onto Truth.

When the mind is at peace, it hooks to the heart.

When the heart is in Love, it hooks to the breath.

When the the breath is with awareness, it hooks to One.

With all of the above hooked,

One get's hooked on to Dhi Truth.

DHI-228
Jan 26 2018 2 pm @Negambo, Sri Lanka

It may take a lifetime to know what is within a breath.

Vice versa, it may take only one breath to know what is within a lifetime.

DHI-229
Feb 4 2018 8 pm @Colombo, Sri Lanka

Thank you for making me
a part of your journey.

DHI-230
Mar 8 2018 9 am @1816zenden

Body-Matter-Physical,
Mind-Intellect-Magnetic,
Breath-Aware-Spiritual:
Are the three planes of existence.

DHI-231
Mar 8 2018 1 pm @1816zenden

All I hopes is to be:
An understanding of your words,
A hug for your thoughts,
A reflection for your ideas.

DHI-232
Mar 10 2018 11 pm @1816zenden

Purpose is over rated,

For it gets lost in Love.

And this Universe is made and built out of Love.

So trying to find the meaning,

Or the purpose of this manifestation,

It may prove futile,

For, at the end one may realize:

It was just a breath at one time.

DHI-233
Mar 14 2018 10 pm @1816zenden

Fighting the fears multiplies them.
Merging them into Love dissolves them.

DHI-234
Mar19 2018 8 am @1816zenden

In accepting the desires versus fighting them,

One awakens to Dhi Truth.

DHI-235
Mar 22 2018 2 pm @1816zenden

If one drops the ego, then all that is left is everything.

DHI-236
Mar 26 2018 4 pm @1816zenden

With each breath one get's ideas.

If the mind catches one, then the heart grabs it from the breath and plants it in the field of Love where everything grows and merges.

If Dhi thinks this idea is important, initially may be for money, then for family and maybe later for community and environment or the universe, this idea will grow in one as long as the lesson in each experience is fed to it.

Each and every idea has a positive, negative and neutral.

Each idea is timeless.

Each idea manifests to change the world.

DHI-237
Apr 3 2018 10 pm @1816zenden

An opportunity to connect at physical, mental, emotional, intellectual and spiritual level has been provided to each and everyone, by Love.

DHI-238
Apt 7 2018 6 pm @1816zenden

When the body, senses and desires are anchored in breath, they reach the mind.

When the mind is anchored in the breath, it reaches the heart.

When the heart is anchored in the breath, it reaches Love.

When Love is anchored in the breath, it reaches the Truth.

When one is anchored in the breath, then Dhi Truth reaches all within the breath.

DHI-239
Apr 15 2018 4 pm @1816zenden

If we follow any words as a thumb rule,
then we are fools.

If we follow a practice as a ritual, then
we will be forsaken.

If we follow in someone's footsteps
thinking it's the path to our destination,
we have lost our way.

Then what is one to do?

Only if we seek the Truth:

then words, practice and footsteps may
help as a guide or navigation points on
the individual unique path that each one
of us was meant to tread.

DHI-240
Apr 24 2018 9 am @1816zenden

When we want to get a particular car or a toy,
we start noticing them all around.

When we want to get a particular house,
we start noticing similar houses.

What ever we seek, we starts noticing or
becoming aware of it.

So when one seek's Love and Truth,
One starts to notice it everywhere, in
everything and within.

DHI-241
Apr 29 2018 8 am @1816zenden

The breath is one's last Guru.

DHI-242
Apr 29 2018 5 pm @1816zenden

As kids we see the world through the eyes of our parents.

As students we start to see via the eyes of our teachers and friends.

Then we start to see via the eyes of our partner.

And when we get old, we see this world through the eyes of our children.

A day may come when one may realize, the ideas that Dhi resonated with, in turn defined the Truth that One saw and pictured.

DHI-243
Apr 30 2018 9 pm @1816zenden

Dhi idea in each religion comes forth when the sacred names are replaced with

"The Truth".

DHI-244
May 1 2018 9 am @1816zenden

Why does a part of me always feel young
no matter what age?

Cause the "Truth" in me never get's old.

DHI-245
May 2 2018. 1 pm @1816zenden

Animals must be thinking look at those people inside entertaining themselves with stuff, fools.

How can they not know everything outside is what is cool.

DHI-246
May 4 2018 10 pm @1816zenden

An apple said to the other apples, "Look at us, we are the most beautiful part of this tree, red as the sun, inside out." Soon, one's time had come, and it fell to the ground. The other apples watched as a bird came and started pecking at the apple, and saw it was all white inside. They all said "aaagh, that is so bad." Soon the birds had eaten the skin, the white and reached the core, where all the other apples said "yikes what is all that black stuff." Seeds you know. The birds had left them to be.

One little apple who had witnessed this act, would wake up every day and see the seeds on the ground and remember the apple that was taken away from the tree. One day the seeds were gone and the little apple didn't know what had happened. In a few days it saw a baby apple tree sprout from that spot.

As this baby tree grew bigger, one day an apple sprouted on the tree, looking exactly like the apple which had fallen to the ground.

The baby apple which had ripened and grown big started laughing and screaming hysterically witnessing this. All other smaller apples asked what happened, to which the Apple said "I saw an Apple fall to the ground and become a part of the birds and become a part of the earth and then grow into this tree you see standing next to us and the apples on that branch." All the young ones thought the old apple had gone nuts except a little one who said "I believe you." To which the old Apple said "My time has come baby. Now keep watching me and see how I become a part of everything you see."

DHI-247
May 6 2018 1 pm @1816zenden

Follow your heart for it knows the way home.

DHI-248
May 9 2018 9 am @1816zenden

The mind perceives what your heart
seeks.

DHI-249
May 9 2018 904 am @1816zenden

If I can exist only in the present then do the past and future also exist only in the present?

DHI-250
May 12 2018 1 am @1816zenden

If the tree grows from a seed, then is the
tree in the seed ?

If the seed comes from the tree, so is the
seed in the tree?

The truth is:

Everything is in everything.

DHI-251
May 12 2018 6 pm @1816zenden

With each breath,
the heart, mind and Truth play.

DHI-252
May 12 2018 8 pm @1816zenden

BALANCE

When balanced we will find Love at
the center.

If I have come into this world to help others,

then have all come into this world to help me?

DHI-253
May 13 2018 1 am @1816zenden

When I leave,
Your tears may come to say goodbye,
But I hope I made you smile
when we had the time.
When I leave,
Flowers may be showered upon me,
But I hope I was never a thorn
when I was by your side.
When I leave,
Some may reflect on memories left
behind,

But I hope when I was,

I reflected the Peace, Love and Truth that
I had.

When I leave,

You may think we have parted for ever,

But remember Love,

We are always one,

Now and hereafter.

DHI-254
May 15 2018 8 pm @1816zenden

If the Sun sees only darkness around him
with no planets to reflect his light or heat,
would he ever become aware of all that
He is.

DHI-255
May 16 2018 12 pm @1816zenden

Just like a baby in the womb is dependent on mom's breath or is a subset of,

One's breath is a subset of earth's breath,

Earth's breath is a subset of sun's,

Sun's breath is a subset of what he is going around.

The breath or time or orbit are all one and the same.

Breath or time is a frequency or vibration that is keeping everything in play.

Each component of the universe or manifestation is breathing at varying lengths, be it physical, intellectual or spiritual.

DHI-256
May 20 2018 1 pm @1816zenden

"As you embark on this journey called life,

remember, you do not have to become anyone,

you were born a masterpiece,

you are the best and there is no one else like you.

Taking one opportunity at a time along the way,

whenever you give your best,

that best in you will be realized, little by little.

And with each choice made,

you may face a resulting win or loss, good or bad,

yes or a no…

But, learning to share the lesson in each experience

irrespective of the result,

will lead you to the best this life has to offer.

Wishing you give the best and learn from the rest as you embark on this journey called life."

DHI-257
May 22 2018 2 pm @1816zenden

The treasures I pursue are hidden in the
moments of Truth.

DHI-258
May 24 2018 6 pm @1816zenden

Priority:

First is health. Second is relationships. Then comes learning.

In other words:

First is i. Then it is all. Finally everything.

In other words:

First the mind. Then the heart. Finally the breath.

In other words:

Peace of mind first. Love in the heart next. Finally:

Truth in learning from each breath.

DHI-259
May 27 2018 12 pm @1816zenden

Acknowledgement leads to acceptance.

Acceptance leads to awareness.

Awareness leads to awakening.

DHI-260
May 28 2018 1am @1816zenden

In the past,

when I showered,

it was to clean the body with soap and water.

Now, when I showers,

along with the body,

thoughts, feelings and ideas are getting cleansed with each breath,

So I feels new and reset.

DHI-261
June 2 2018 10 am @1816zenden

When I searched for peace,

I found it

by the beach,

on top of the mountain,

in the new car, home and bank
balance,

or in a moment that I called my
own.

Then in my pursuit to have more
of it,

I tried to find this source of my
peace,

only to see my journey end within,

In which lay the source:

My Dhi.

DHI-262
Jun 4 2018 1 pm @1816zenden

When I searched for Love,

I found it:

with my friends in crime,

with my family from one blood,

with strangers in a moment I
cannot explain.

Then in my pursuit to have
more of it,

I tried to find the source of this
Love of mine,

Only to realize I was back in
the familiar place,

Deep within,

Is where the source of Love
hid,

From where all had manifested
to begin with.

DHI-263
Jun 4 2018 1 pm @1816zenden

When I searched for Truth,
Camouflaged within all the lies
and desires,
I found it right here in the now.
To be with it more,
I travelled to places unknown.
Then with a smile,
I sat in my chair at home.
In the bustle of it all,
I had found what my heart and
mind were looking for,
As usual,
Right under my nose.
In each breath
was everything that I ever seeks.

DHI-264
Jun 4 2018 3 pm @1816zenden

Abhi means "here and
now" in Hindi.

So when asked:

Who are you?

I say: Abhi

Where are you from?

Abhi

When did you get here?

Abhi

Where do you live?

Abhi

What do you pursue?

Abhi

Where are you going?

Abhi

Where is peace, love and
truth?

Abhi

DHI-265
Jun 17 2018 10 am @1816zenden

I keep going around in circles
day in day out.
When the time comes to rest,
I realize the opportunity which may have
been lost.
With everyday it came,
This opportunity to reflect,
The opportunity to give,
The opportunity to look within.
And as I sit here,
I finally see what I was seeking,
Hiding in each breath.

DHI-266
Jun 24 2018 11 pm @1816zenden

The cosmic manifestation,
they say, it came from the
cosmic intelligence.

The cosmic intelligence, they
say, it came from the
cosmic consciousness.

And what one calls Dhi, it is
all the three:
Manifestation, Intelligence
and Consciousness in play,

In the single moment of
Truth per se.

DHI-267
Jun 28 2018 9 am @1816zenden

If I seeks Truth then what is Truth
seeking?

DHI-268
Jun 28 2018 6 pm @1816zenden

When the apple realizes, that it was the seed with no color taste or smell at its center that produced the branches, the leaves, the roots and the fruit with this seed inside, the apple may become a little more appreciative of who actually made it or of it's source.

The fact that the seed reacted with earth, water, sun, air and ether to make everything, may generate a sense of humbleness in the realized apple.

Once realized and accepted, it is inevitable for the apple to see how everything is alive and conscious in proportion within a particular dimension and intelligence.

With the physical chemical and magnetic aspects clearer, it is inevitable for the beautiful tasty apple to see the big picture of how the seed connected to the sun, moon and earth to transforms itself into the tree that produces the apple containing the seed, over and over again in a circle.

Dhi, the faculty in one that resonates, ever remains it self through the transmigration from one state to the other only to aid a growth for a better state in the coming opportunity.

DHI-269
Jul 2 2018 1 pm @1816zenden

The east may tend to focus on the essence of the power of the heart and emotions.

The west may tend to focus on the essence of the power of the mind and logic.

But it is when Dhi embraces both, we realize the essence of how the heart and mind are connected in the breath.

DHI-270
Jul 4 2018 9 pm @1816zenden

Listen my sanity and ego,
everything is beyond your control.
I share my Love with you in a hope,
that you may learn to let go,
and merge with the One that
you will never know.

DHI-271
Jul 5 2018 9 pm @1816zenden

These words that flow,
I know them not to be
from my comprehension.
They have come to me
for the one reason:
To be set free,
So others too may conceive
their true meaning
in their own Dhi.

DHI-272
Jul 8 2018 1 pm @1816zenden

I is able to be the best in front of you,
because my loved ones
have put up with my worst,
day in day out.

DHI-273
Jul 9 2018 11 pm @1816zenden

In marriage, no matter what, there seems to be a room for improvement until "death do us apart".

So why go through this experience one may ask?

Schooling may teach us working with a desire and for a particular result.

But making a family will teach one about responsibility, acceptance and giving the best to all with Love.

DHI-274
Jul 10 2018 9 am @1816zenden

The truth that manifests in the mind is in the form of idea.

The truth that manifests in the heart is in the form of love.

The truth that manifests in the breath is in the form of awareness.

As one becomes a witness to all the above,

One resonates with Dhi Truth in each moment.

DHI-275
Jul 14 2018 10 am @1816zenden

I connected to those I know with desires
and wants.
Then I connected to all with Love.
Finally I connected to the universe in the
Truth.
And now I see,
that it is the Truth that manifested into
Love and then into desire.
Each relationship manifests deeper or
shallower day by day depending on
where Dhi is:

Desire, Love or Truth.

DHI-276
Jul 20 2018 1 pm @1816zenden

OPEN:

In being open and oneself we befriend
Love.

Mirror is the most enlightening thing
that I have seen, because it reflects the
ever young Truth in you and me.

DHI-277
Jul 19 2018 9 pm @1816zenden

The Truth in each desire is Idea.
The Truth in the idea is Love.
The Truth in Love is Awareness.
The Truth in Awareness is One.

DHI-278
Jul 20 2018 7 pm @1816zenden

A circle is infinite for it has no start nor
an end.

DHI-279
Jul 24 2018 2 pm @1816zenden

Where is my destiny when there is
nowhere left to go?

DHI-280
Jul 24 2018 7 pm @1816zenden

The shape of Truth is a circle because its refection always remains a circle.

DHI-281
Jul 27 2018 1 pm @1816zenden

Did the Truth mask it self in a lie so it
may come to know what is the difference
between the opposites.

DHI-282
Jul 28 2018 8 am @1816zenden

My acts which yield gold or dirt,
They don't mean anything in my world.
For, where I lives with my Love,
Everything is just One.

DHI-283
Jul 29 2018 12 pm @1816zenden

What is the difference between Attention, Awareness, Witness and the Truth?

DHI-284
Jul 30 2018 2 pm @1816zenden

They say it is mother earth who carries all our weight on her shoulders. The heaviness being directly proportional to how conscious one is, unconscious being the heaviest.
One may make the load lighter by becoming a little more conscious and aware each day: be it physical, mindful or spiritual.

DHI-285
Aug 5 2018 11 pm @1816zenden

As I rambled on about some idea a few months ago, my wife says:

"Only with Love:

My home becomes my temple.

My kids become my celebration (puja).

My work becomes my purpose (sadhana).

My family becomes One."

DHI-286
Aug 7 2018 1 pm @1816zenden

Without love it is like having a billion
dollars without the "One".

DHI-287
Aug 12 2018 9 am @1816zenden

Whenever one is the true self,
Be it with someone or in a situation,
Then are they in true Love?

DHI-288
Aug 14 2018 3 pm @1816zenden

True self is when
what one thinks, speaks and does
is in synch with Dhi intent.

DHI-289
Aug 15 2018 11 pm @1816zenden

If I am in Love then what is Love in?

DHI-290
Aug 17 2018 1 am @1816zenden

My desire is to do everything
without a desire.

DHI-291
Aug 18 2018 2 pm @1816zenden

Congrats on all the new beginnings that started last year.

Wishing they grow to meet your ideas for this year.

DHI-292
Aug 20 2018 9 am @1816zenden

My tears roll down the cheeks, so a tickle
may arise to cause a smile.

DHI-293
Aug 27 2018 4 pm @1816zenden

My breath comes in to take the shape of
Dhi and then spreads in to the world
around me.

DHI-294
Aug 29 2018 5 pm @1816zenden

Two conflicting thoughts may dissolve
only in Love.

DHI-295
Sep 2 2018 8 am @1816zenden

Ideas are born out of Love and dissolve
in Love.

DHI-296
Sep 4 2018 11 am @1816zenden

Love is made in Truth.

DHI-297
Sep 5 2018 4 pm @1816zenden

Is a stone aware that it is a stone?
Is a bird aware that it is a bird?
Am I aware of who I is?

DHI-298
Sep 9 2018 9 am @1816zenden

Dinner table discussion points for family and friends:

Health vs Wealth

Family vs Career

Teachers vs Mentors

Politics vs Personal

Mother vs Father

Boys vs Girls

Strangers vs Friends

Good vs Bad

Love vs Fear

Compassion vs Hate

Best vs whatever

Religion vs Science

Birth vs Death

Now vs Past vs Future

Ethics vs Education

Meditation vs Addiction

Values vs Skills

Running vs Endorphin

Honesty vs Lies

Greed vs Content

Pampering vs Parenting

Responsibility vs Reckless

Respect vs Insult

Patience vs Instant

Roots vs Fruits

Actual vs Imagination

DHI-299
Sep 14 2018 11 am @1816zenden

Who makes the choice: is it my ego, my mind, my Dhi or my love or my awareness?

DHI-300
Sep 18 2018 11 am @1816zenden

LEARN:

In Love, we open up to learning new
lessons.

Balanced ideas help one and all with
Love, in Love and for Love.

DHI-301
Sep 20 2018 10 am @1816zenden

Love fills the heart which is open in acceptance to help share the best one has within.

DHI-302
Sep 20 2018 10 am @1816zenden

From awareness in each breath one learns
the Truth in each moment.

DHI-303
Sep 20 2018 10 am @1816zenden

With each breath, awareness flows to the heart and attention flows to the mind.

DHI-304
Sep 22 2018 10 am @1816zenden

Catch me if you can is what the mind
said to the breath.

DHI-305
Sep 24 2018 2 pm @1816zenden

Do ideas hide in the mind?
Does Love hide in the heart?
Does awareness hide in the breath?

DHI-306
Sep 25 2018 1 pm @1816zenden

Going with the flow is the trait of awareness since it knows how to float in each breath.

DHI-307
Sep 27 2018 1.30 pm @1816zenden

I may be angry or happy or sad or joyous
or ..

But in awareness I merges to become one
with the breath and float along in bliss.

DHI-308
Sep 29 2018 202 pm @1816zenden

Thinking addiction is the worst of them all, since our mind concerns with matters that don't matter.

DHI-309
Sep 30 2018 3 pm @1816zenden

If my past and future are merged into the
now, then where will I be?

DHI-310
Oct 1 2018 12 pm @1816zenden

What one seeks to feel,
What one seeks to see,
What one seeks to taste,
Whatever one seeks out of this
opportunity called life,
I say,
It has always been with me,
hiding in each moment
that has been called:
The breath of I.

DHI-311
Oct 26 2018 9 am @1816zenden

They took me to what they called
home of The One.

Standing outside,

Some one said "wow look at the
color of the wall",

and another said "wow the roof
looks so strong",

One from the side view said "wow I
smell something so awesome",

And I asked "has anyone been
inside my friend?"

To which they said "no questions
do you understand, just do as we
say and obey."

This went on for years, I tried to
follow suit, work hard, family,
beliefs and values.

One day, Dawn knocked at my door.

I could not see no light , hear no sound, smell no fragrance, seemed like I was maybe half gone.

But I found my self in front of this home of The One I had previously gone.

I looked around and no one was there, so I opened the door and stepped in to this forbidden place for me, they had said.

I found the walls so beautiful made out of glass that reflected me in everything outside.

As I walked around, it was just peace, it was just love, it was just bliss.

For the first time in my life I felt alive.

And slowly when my gaze shifted to the sun rising in a distance.

Through these glass walls I could see the sun, the beautiful mountains, ocean and the breath of the breeze,

For the first time I saw how my own reflection fit perfectly in the beautiful scene.

And slowly but surely this thought started to creep up through my veins:

I want to stay here forever. This is my home. Let me lock the door so no one disturbs me here in my abode.

In that single thought that felt eternal,

I was jolted and thrown out to land back in my bed.

Was it a dream I wondered as I
looked outside the window of my
bedroom as I lay,

To see the yellow flower sway in the
breeze,

and again saw how my reflection in
the glass window fit in perfectly

with the world that was waiting

for me here in this moment

called "my home".

DHI-312
Oct 29 2018 11 am @1816zendenn

When we let the words we say,
Sink to the deepest depths,
They will merge with Love,
So we may live them as part of
our breath.

DHI-313
Nov 1 2018 11 am @1816zenden

Love is the connection between the manifested world and the Truth.

Love is the only doorway through which one may pass between the spiritual and physical world.

When all religious teaching emphasize Love, the objective may have been to ensure we will be the best in our responsibilities and reach our destiny; Love being in the middle of the Truth and the world we manifest.

Dhi Thesis:

Love is the one from whose branches sprout to go higher and higher to bloom the reality in this physical realm and the roots go deeper and deeper to the Truth from which all manifestations are nourished.

DHI-314
Nov 2 2018 12 pm @1816zenden

If I know the Truth then does Truth
know me?

DHI-315
Nov 3 2018 12 pm @1816zendenn

If I become aware in my sleep of the
dream I am dreaming, then am I awake
or in a dream?

DHI-316
Nov 4 2018 2 pm @1816zenden

If there is Truth in everything
and everything is in the Truth
then what is the Truth?

DHI-317
Nov 6 2018 7 pm @1816zenden

Thought I was this amazing
red being

Hanging around, acting cool
and swaying with the wind.

I grew and grew to the best I
could be

to all would say " look at him,
he is what we need to be."

When the time came I fell to
the green.

My family and friends cried
cause I was no longer to be
seen.

As I lay on the ground , I could
see for the very first time,

The tall tree, its branches,
leaves , my brothers and sisters
and the connection I had left
behind.

As I lay there,

Wondering was this my destiny,
to become ripe for the picking
and fall onto the green?

A bird flew down and took a
piece of me.

I felt no pain as I became a
part of this bird.

Then a ground worm took a
piece too.

And soon, what I had claimed
to be this mighty red fruit
called "me",

was all gone and not to be seen.

Except the seed that now lay
alone.

Is this really me, tasteless and
ugly within?

I thought and analyzed.

Time passed in this state of
analysis.

Then came the rains the sun
the wind and the earth,
breaking this last piece of so
called Me.

Was this the end finally ?

And as they tore open the shell
of the seed,
I was finally free.
And I danced with the sun,
And I danced with the wind,
And the water and the earth
dear.
And when the dance had
ended,
I saw my self in the reflection
of the water,
I had become a small Apple
tree,

A little away from the one that
I had fallen from.
As I grew,
I grew the roots the shoots the
leaves and finally the fruit with
a seed within.

So who am I?

The tree, the shoot, the fruit,
leaves, roots, sun, wind, air,
water or the seed..

I heard a voice say:

I am all what my Dhi choses on
be'ing.

DHI-318
Nov 8 2018 1 pm @1816zenden

If I work to give my best, accept the rest
and learn from whatever I get, then am I
in Love with my work ?

DHI-319
Nov 8 2018 9 pm @1816zenden

If truth of the matter is in the
mind then where is the truth of
the mind ?

DHI-320
Nov 10 2018 1 pm @1816zenden

If the Truth in you and me in one, then
who is who?

DHI-321
Nov 10 2018 1 pm @1816zenden

If destiny puts me in harms way, then is
the chosen path my destiny?

DHI-322
Nov 12 2018 2 pm @1816zenden

Is the Truth in Love called true love?

DHI-323
Nov 13 2018 9 pm @1816zenden

Is it a desire,
If it is a desire to be with the Truth in
the now and forever?

DHI-324
Nov 14 2018 9 am @1816zenden

DHI CREDITS

Everything in this book, be it the ideas, thoughts, concepts, stories, songs, perspectives and knowledge have been written, sung and communicated by many over the past centuries in their own context.

So what is emphasized in this effort is not original in any form or fashion except from the perspective of Dhi.

Hope we comprehend the words conveyed in their truest essence.

Respect.
Abhi DhiYogi

Oct 16th 2016 6 pm @1816zenden